On Weathering

On Weathering

The Life of Buildings in Time

Mohsen Mostafavi and David Leatherbarrow

The MIT Press

Cambridge, Massachusetts

London, England

This book was set in Bembo and Futura by DEKR Corporation and was printed and bound in the United States of America.

Library of Congress Cataloging-in-Publication Data

Mostafavi, Mohsen.
    On weathering : the life of buildings in time / Mohsen Mostafavi and David Leatherbarrow.
        p.   cm.
    Includes bibliographical references.
    ISBN 0-262-13291-5. — ISBN 0-262-63144-X (pbk.)
    1. Weathering of buildings.   I. Leatherbarrow, David.   II. Title.
TH9039.M67   1993
720′.28′8—dc20   92-30318
                                                                    CIP

To Neda, Sara, and Ethan

CONTENTS

On Weathering

FOR TO END YET AGAIN

SAMUEL BECKETT

THE WATER HOLLOWED THE STONE,
THE WIND DISPERSED THE WATER,
THE STONE STOPPED THE WIND.
WATER AND WIND AND STONE.

OCTAVIO PAZ, *A DRAFT OF SHADOWS*

Finishing ends construction, weathering constructs finishes.

————————————————

This assertion would seem to defy one of the most ancient commonplaces of architecture: buildings persist in time. Yet they do not. No building stands forever, eventually every one falls under the influence of the elements, and this end is known from the beginning. How, then, can one say weathering "constructs" finishes when the action of the elements leads to the deterioration of the building? Weathering does not construct, it destroys.

Over time the natural environment acts upon the outer surface of a building in such a way that its underlying materials are broken down. This breakdown, when left to proceed un-interrupted, leads to the failure of materials and the final dis-solution of the building itself—ruination—hardly an outcome desired by the architect, builder, or owner. In order to prevent this or retard its occurrence buildings must be maintained. Maintenance, in most general terms, aims at renewal and in-volves both conservation and replacement. So costly has this process become nowadays that buildings are designed to be maintenance-free, or to require as little repair as possible. Nevertheless, no matter how maintenance-free the construc-tion, weathering still occurs. Perhaps, then, there is some truth to Victor Hugo's famous argument that buildings are less durable than books, that the "dominant idea of each generation" will be embodied in the book of paper rather than the book of stone, the first being more enduring because ubiquitous, the second being less durable because unique and more costly.[1] Buildings are single substantial structures that can be demolished by men or nature or both in time. In architecture, the gradual destruction of buildings by nature in time is weathering.

In the mathematics of the environment weathering is a power of subtraction, a *minus*, under the sign of which newly finished corners, surfaces, and colors are "taken away" by rain, wind, and sun. But is weathering only subtraction, can it not also *add* and enhance? Deleterious consequences can be complemented by the potential value of sedimentation and the accumulation of detritus on a surface through the action of the weather. This process always marks, and these marks may be intended, even desired. This sense of weathering is often associated with a romantic appreciation of the appearance of buildings that have aged: their mellowed brickwork, moss-covered stone, and seasoned timber. A fascination with ruins was common throughout the late eighteenth and nineteenth centuries. This theme appears very frequently in painting, literature, aesthetics, and architecture. In ancient buildings marks of the environment are added, leaving residual deposits

Villa Savoye (1928–1931), after restoration
Le Corbusier
Poissy-sur-Seine, France

Villa Savoye (1928–1931), before restoration
Le Corbusier
Poissy-sur-Seine, France

Palazzo Chiericati (1550–1580), weathered column
Andrea Palladio
Vicenza, Italy

Sanatorium Zonnestraal (1926–1931)
J. Duiker, B. Bijvoet, J. G. Wiebenga
Hilversum, Netherlands

Nirvana Flats (1927–1929)
J. Duiker, J. G. Wiebenga
The Hague, Netherlands

40 Corso Venezia
Milan, Italy

Bibliothèque Sainte-Geneviève (1838–1850)
Henri Labrouste
Paris, France

Casa del Girasole (1947–1950)
Luigi Moretti
Rome, Italy

House, weathered wall
Poggiana, Italy

that reveal through traces the coherence of ambient elements on a surface. In the process of subtracting the "finish" of a construction, weathering adds the "finish" of the environment. Subtraction leads to final ruination and intimates, therefore, the end of the building as it would the death of the figure. Aging, then, can be seen as either benign or tragic—or as both. This raises a question: beyond the general category of weathering as a romantic form of aging, are there other specific ways the unending process of deterioration can be understood, and then intended? Is it possible that weathering is not only a problem to be solved, or a fact to be neglected, but is an inevitable occurrence to be recognized and made use of in the uncertainties of its manifestation?

Our aim in the argument that follows is to revise the sense of the ending of an architectural project, not to see finishing as the final moment of construction but to see the unending deterioration of a finish that results from weathering, the continuous metamorphosis of the building itself, as part of its beginning(s) and its ever-changing "finish."

———————————

The fact of weathering as deterioration has often been associated with modern architecture. The house as "machine for living," Le Corbusier's emblem of a new spirit of equality between the classes, was to be achieved through mass production, and because of this was to be "healthy (and morally so too) and beautiful in the same way that the working tools and instruments that accompany our existence are beautiful."[2] Mass production, and the ensuing changes in methods of assembly determined by this new aesthetic, were, nevertheless, to be the source of a great degree of unpredictability in the life of buildings after construction.

This unpredictability was a result not only of a lack of experience in new methods of assembly, but also of the use of both new and traditional materials in unprecedented and varying proportions.[3] The use of these varying proportions was to challenge the traditional relationship between larger, more permanent elements and smaller, replaceable parts (frames, doors, windows, etc.). In many modern buildings the number of replaceable parts exceeded those of traditional buildings. This was especially true in larger buildings where the load-bearing structure was enveloped by either light or heavy cladding, analogous to the relationship between the corresponding parts of automobiles. Architectural parts, however, could not always be replaced easily, so were not; more common was the *appearance* of possible replacement. The increase in the number of parts went hand in hand with the increase in the number of joints, or points of connection between elements—joints by juxtaposition rather than synthesis. Connections of this sort were usually made weather-tight with sealants, which were

Asilo d'Infanza Sant'Elia (1935–1937)
Giuseppe Terragni
Como, Italy

DELAGE, 1921

If the problem of the dwelling or the flat were studied in the same way that a chassis is, a speedy transformation and improvement would be seen in our houses. If houses were constructed by industrial mass-production, like chassis, unexpected but sane and defensible forms would soon appear, and a new æsthetic would be formulated with astonishing precision.

There is a new spirit: it is a spirit of construction and of synthesis guided by clear conception.

Programme of *l'Esprit Nouveau.*
No. 1. October 1920.

IT is necessary to press on towards the establishment of *standards* in order to face the problem of *perfection.*

The Parthenon is a product of selection applied to an established standard. Already for a century the Greek temple had been standardized in all its parts.

Delage automobile (1921)
from Le Corbusier, *Towards a New Architecture*

Sports Center
Lyons, France

not always effective in allowing for structural movements. This resulted in an increased number of places in the building exposed to the influence of the elements.

The impact of mechanization, in relation to the building industry, necessitated the provision of a larger body of information by the architect to the builder, as these things could not be left to chance. The increasing utilization of both electricity and plumbing exemplifies the tendency toward specialization and the carrying out of building projects according to the manufacturer's specifications as well as previously established standards of production.[4] These standards, instituted by official bodies, were seen as a way of safeguarding for the consumer the qualities of production and execution. New standards were complemented by new graphic documents executed by the architect. The supposed freedom to invent had the natural consequence of exposing the limitations of invention.

Architecture made out of a greater number of mass-produced parts also changed the relationship between the architect and the builder by largely reducing the role of the latter's knowledge of traditional ways of building and relying upon construction procedures almost entirely prescribed by the architect. Independent of the architect's instructions for assembly, construction could not proceed. Insufficient instructions by the architect, and poor workmanship by the builder,

The Growing House (exhibition, 1932), section
Walter Gropius
Berlin, Germany

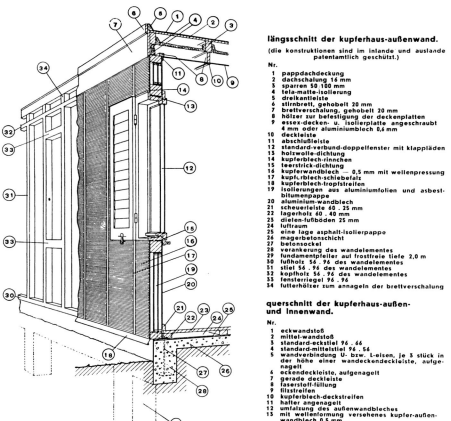

längsschnitt der kupferhaus-außenwand.
(die konstruktionen sind im inlande und auslande
    patentamtlich geschützt.)

Nr.

1   pappdachdeckung
2   dachschalung 16 mm
3   sparren 50/100 mm
4   tela-matte-isolierung
5   dreikantleiste
6   stirnbrett, gehobelt 20 mm
7   brettverschalung, gehobelt 20 mm
8   hölzer zur befestigung der deckenplatten
9   essex-decken- u. isolierplatte angeschraubt
    4 mm oder aluminiumblech 0,6 mm
10 deckleiste
11 abschlußleiste
12 standard-verbund-doppelfenster mit klappläden
13 holzwolle-dichtung
14 kupferblech-rinnchen
15 teerstrick-dichtung
16 kupferwandblech — 0,5 mm mit wellenpressung
17 kupferblech-schiebefalz
18 kupferblech-tropfstreifen
19 isolierungen aus aluminiumfolien und asbest-
    bitumenpappe
20 aluminium-wandblech
21 scheuerleiste 60 . 25 mm
22 lagerholz 60 . 40 mm
23 dielen-fußböden 25 mm
24 luftraum
25 eine lage asphalt-isolierpappe
26 magerbetonschicht
27 betonsockel
28 verankerung des wandelementes
29 fundamentpfeiler auf frostfreie tiefe 2,0 m
30 fußholz 56 . 96 des wandelementes
31 stiel 56 . 96 des wandelementes
32 kopfholz 56 . 96 des wandelementes
33 fensterriegel 96 . 96
34 futterhölzer zum annageln der brettverschalung

**querschnitt der kupferhaus-außen-
und innenwand.**

Nr.

1   eckwandstoß
2   mittel-wandstoß
3   standard-eckstiel 96 . 66
4   standard-mittelstiel 96 . 56
5   wandverbindung U- bzw. L-eisen, je 3 stück in
    der höhe einer wandeckendeckleiste, aufge-
    nagelt
6   eckendeckleiste, aufgenagelt
7   gerade deckleiste
8   faserstoff-füllung
9   filzstreifen
10 kupferblech-deckstreifen
11 hafter angenagelt
12 umfalzung des außenwandbleches
13 mit wellenformung versehenes kupfer-außen-
    wandblech 0,5 mm
14 1 lage asbest-bitumenpappe
15 1 lage aluminium-folie
16 2 lagen aluminium-folie
17 2 lagen asbest-bitumenpappe mit 1 lage alu-
    miniumfolie dazwischen
18 mit wellenpressung versehenes aluminium-
    innenblech
19 holzleiste zum anfügen der isolierungen
20 innenwandblechstoß
21 stumpfer wandstoß
22 wandverbindungseisen je 3 stück in der höhe
    einer wand
23 filzstreifen
24 standard-fensterstiel 96 . 96
25 standard verbund-doppelfenster
26 holzwolledichtung
27 klappläden

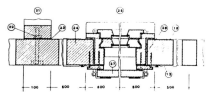

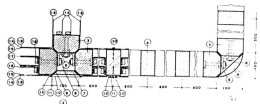

die konstruktionen sind im in- und
auslande durch patente geschützt

were among the principal causes of material deterioration in buildings. This subordination of builder to architect in construction inverted their roles. Previously "gentlemen architects" had relied upon the builder's knowledge when undertaking building projects.[5] The elimination of the builder's traditional role exacerbated the difficulty of assembly and of anticipating the life of the construction under the elements.

The frequency of material failure due to weathering in early modern buildings has led, in more recent times, to the construction of buildings that are more efficient and more resistant to deterioration through weathering. Efficient buildings are achieved in contemporary practice on the basis of a particular aspect of the construction process: architects who have designed in diagrams instruct construction supervisors in procedures to be implemented by builders. Influential in this restructuring has been another kind of efficiency, the economy of capital investment. Two results have followed: one, the reduction of the time of construction, shortening the interval between the project's inception and its potential occupancy; two, the following of construction procedures that use mass-produced parts and techniques developed in the modern movement, independent of its social and political aspirations. These procedures, together with the expectation of speedy efficiency, have affected architectural production at each of its stages. At the design stage all necessary documents must be prepared

Airoh aluminum house (1948)
London, England

quickly, which often results in the repetitive use of details and specifications with as little modification as possible. This saves time and money, and reduces risk in construction on account of unfamiliarity. But this is ironic: mass production, which promises greater choice, has come in current practice to favor formulaic solutions. Still greater changes have resulted from the use of computers and more automated modes of production. Computers have unprecedented capacity for information storage, the advantage of which is ease of both repetition and modification of designs or details based upon this information; yet the ease of repetition seems to have increased instances of unmodified repetition and reduced reinvention.[6]

These changes, however, have been greater in some countries than in others. The Portuguese architect Alvaro Siza, writing about his doubts about using the same architectural materials throughout Europe, has observed the differences between selection and assembly in Portugal and Holland.[7] In Holland choices are multiple, limited only by cost. So many choices exist that there is little chance for building up experience with any one of them, except through repetition. By contrast, fewer choices exist in Portugal because fewer materials are available; as a result, more experience with the materials can be gained. The abstract sense of materials built up in Holland is achieved through trade books, product literature, and computerized information. This has manifested itself, ac-

Dymaxion Deployment Unit (1940–1941)
Buckminster Fuller

Cité de Refuge de l'Armée du Salut (1929–1933), original facade
Le Corbusier
Paris, France

Cité de Refuge de l'Armée du Salut (1929–1933), facade shades
Le Corbusier
Paris, France

cording to Siza, in buildings being "glued together . . . until the first storms lay bare what could have been foreseen."[8] Material failure varies from place to place. The use of the same technologies throughout the world does not always take the uniqueness of places into account.

Architecture made up of a "kit of parts" changed the relationship between a building and its potential site, allowing assembly and construction to take place on any site, to a great degree independent of its local environmental and climatic conditions—which paradoxically makes it siteless. The variations in the weather and hence in weathering, which can be anticipated in any location, cannot be reconciled with this manner of practice. Older architectures also composed elements shaped after preexisting forms; what is unique in modern practice is the increased proportion of elements of this kind, and the corresponding reduction of elements that allow pregiven forms to be reconciled with a given location. This practice, among other things, has motivated much criticism in recent years, an example of which is Aldo Rossi's argument on the making of a site through the introduction of pregiven forms. This results, Rossi argues, in the *remaking* of the site, designated by the term *locus*.

Le Corbusier, however, intended a single building for all nations and climates. His ideal of "the well-tempered environment" was to be achieved through *respiration exacte* in all locations; every building was to maintain a temperature of 18 degrees centigrade throughout its interior all year long.[9] In a section of *The Radiant City* called "Exact Respiration" Le Corbusier observed "the discovery that if architecture follows certain paths, it can provide city dwellers with good, true, God-given air, for the salvation of their lungs." This observation rested upon biological fact (Le Corbusier cited measures of air through the body per hour and bacteria counts for the Rue de Rivoli) but elaborated a program of salvation: "the air of the cities is not God-given, it is the devil's air." A consequence of "the building for all nations" was the clear distinction between inside and outside made possible by the *mur neutralisant*, a double skin wall with services passing between its layers, creating a sealed environment, like a "space capsule," says Banham, but without the pragmatic benefits of air conditioning devised by Willis Carrier, and seen by Le Corbusier when he visited the United States in 1935–1936.[10] In effect there were two circuits of air, one within the glazing system and another within the enclosed volume of the building, the latter being the one that was to be kept clean, "ozonified," and at a constant temperature and humidity. So closed was this skin to be that Le Corbusier would tolerate no openings, with the exception of "portholes," through which tenants could lean out.

Flatness was a result of this desire for an environment that was meant to be controlled, therapeutic, and iconic; the ambient air (with all its qualities) became a principle of life and the building an authentic *Cité de Refuge*. As built, the facade had specific characteristics, the consequences of which, from the point of view of weathering, were the elimination of external elements designed specifically to retard deterioration through the regulation of the action of water on surfaces, and the impossibility of controlling heat gain and loss through operable windows. In the Salvation Army building in Paris, Le Corbusier's glass facade, originally intended as a "neutralizing wall," was, due to budgetary restrictions, constructed of a sheet of single-pane glass, which utterly failed to maintain an 18-degree temperature within.[11] The sealed wall of glass, oriented as it was on its site, worked like a greenhouse in the summer. Eventually, the planning authorities forced the fitting of operable windows, *fenêtres d'illusion*, later to be supplemented with the addition of external shades. These reduced solar heat gain by making the glass wall more congenial to its location, despite the architect's disapproval. The history of this window, from its invention to its failure and final modification, illustrates the difficulties of inventing everything—all over again. Nevertheless, such cases can lead to new solutions.

The breakdown or breakup of materials as a result of weathering might be called "functional deterioration." More commonly lamented in the criticism of modern architecture, however, is the modification to surfaces through erosion and the accumulation of dirt from weathering—staining—which is a physical fact that carries ethical implications. This form of surface modification might be called "aesthetic" deterioration, as it can make buildings either "sightly" or "unsightly."[12] Unsightly weathering occurs when stains due to the washing effect of rainwater or to the appearance of dirt and soot are concentrated on specific areas of an architectural surface. These consequences are accentuated through the inadequate provision of projections for regulating the downward flow of water: sills, copings, downpipes, and similar details, a common inadequacy of "flat" facades. This results in disfiguration, particularly of surfaces built from more porous materials, such as limestone and concrete. Not only does rainwater deposit residue from the air or nearby soil, it can also leave traces of soluble salts from other materials of a construction—especially those situated above a porous surface. Dirt carried by the wind is deposited in cracks parallel to the ground level, and on flat surfaces above the ground level. This accumulation, together with stains made from rainwater, can dramatically change the overall appearance of a building.

Deterioration was retarded in traditional buildings through the incorporation of elements that restricted direct exposure to rainwater. This was understood in modern architecture as well; in *Oeuvre Complète* Le Corbusier quoted with approval Perret's dictum "L'ornement . . . cache toujours une

Street near the Asilo Sant'Elia
Como, Italy

Maison du Peuple (1937–1939)
Jean Prouvé with E. Beaudoin, V. Bodiansky, M. G. Lods
Clichy, France

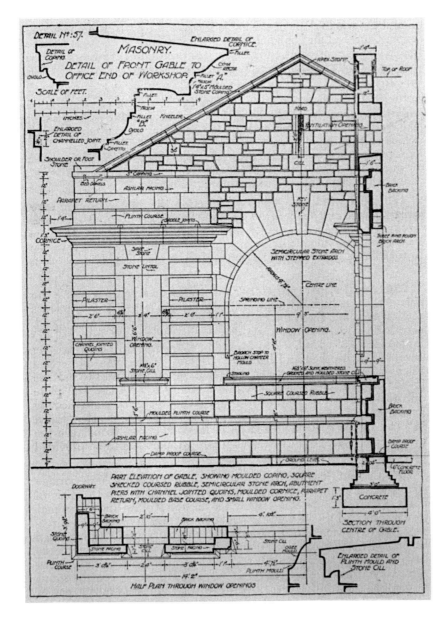

Gable detail showing "drip"
from W. R. Jaggard, *Architectural Building Construction*

faute de construction." Accordingly, he tried to eliminate faults. Restricted exposure and retarded deterioration, as well as the use of larger areas of a single material, tended to prolong the life of buildings. The term "weathering" was, in fact, originally defined as that part of a building that projected beyond the surface of any external wall and served as a "drip," in order to throw off rainwater. Weathering also referred to a sloped "setoff" of a wall or buttress, or the inclination of any surface, designed to prevent the lodgement of water. This sense of the term survives in present usage in the terms "weather-board," "weatherstrip," and "weatherproofing." Generally speaking, whatever controls the action of the weather is referred to as the "weathering"—one word naming both the *process* and the *object* through which this process is controlled and allowed to make itself manifest. Elements fashioned to retard deterioration (sills, cornices, copings—"weatherings" of all sorts) were incorporated into the design of all traditional and some modern buildings. In many instances weathering shapes were transferred from one material to another, from stone to tin sheeting for example. Although always specified in traditional design, these elements were sometimes removed in modern construction, which brought the need for new sealants. In pursuit of the "always new," weatherproofing has replaced weatherings. The shape of weathering elements was as important as the materials out of which they were made;

Rue Colbert
Paris, France

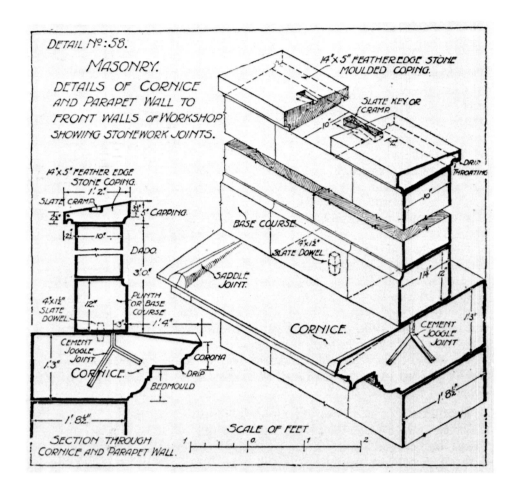

Cornice detail showing "weatherings"
from W. R. Jaggard, *Architectural Building Construction*

likewise the way they were bonded together. When stones were laid, the strongest side of the stone was to be placed where the wall was exposed to the weather. It was discovered that stones should not be placed on their sides, with the grain pointing upward, but horizontally, in order to prevent pressure from the load above from cracking the stone. Correct placement in the wall was also affected by the stone's location in a quarry: stone with its grain facing inward in the quarry was to be placed facing outward in the building and was most resistant when cut transversely across its grain. Thus the placement of stone in construction recalls the stone's origins in cutting and anticipates its aging in weathering.

The use of moldings and recesses, intended to retard surface deterioration, nevertheless resulted in staining, the formation of the soot and whitewash effect. This was common, even inevitable, in stone buildings. It has been plausibly suggested that this whitewash effect was intended to create a simultaneity of light and shade on a building's facade. Examples of this in Venetian architecture are many; a good case is the Palazzo Ducale.

Creation in this sense is the work of an architect and builder anticipating the work of the elements. The contrast between light and dark on a building surface provides it with shadows permanently embedded within its fabric. The contrast between light and dark is also an opposition between distinct

Palazzo Ducale (1340–1419)
Filippo Calendario
Venice, Italy

De Bijenkorf Department Store (1955–1957)
Marcel Breuer, A. Elzas
Rotterdam, Netherlands

and indefinite, and a tension between actual and virtual. Palladio's work elaborates these oppositions, as does Michelangelo's, whose sketches and writings further extend the topic into an antithesis between spirit and matter, manifested in "live" and "dead" stone. While it may be possible to see all weathering as deterioration, the production of distracting marks that dirty original surfaces, this recognition of the play of shadows and the inevitability of marking suggests an alternative interpretation, one of weathering as a process that can productively modify a building over time.

It may not be possible to separate this sense of aging from an awareness of the future dissolution of a building as a result of the very processes that have modified its surface. From one point of view, then, the accumulation of dirt enriches; from another, it dissolves the building. The first, if uninterrupted, leads to the second.

The facade of the *cortile* of the Palazzo del Tè, prior to its most recent restoration, was a perfect example of an architecture wearing its own "death mask."[13] Perhaps its deterioration was anticipated by Giulio Romano. The question hinges on an interpretation of the relationship between anticipation of weathering and the use of "unfinished" materials. Exterior surfaces vary from place to place in the Palazzo and its gardens. The conditions of the exterior surfaces after the restoration are very different in character from those of Romano's original

Palazzo Massimo alle Colonne (begun 1532)
Baldassarre Peruzzi
Rome, Italy

Sant'Andrea (1472–1514)
Leon Battista Alberti
Mantua, Italy

Sacré-Coeur (1872–1912)
Paul Abadie
Paris, France

Palazzo del Tè (1526)
Giulio Romano
Mantua, Italy

construction. Yet the columns that line the entry passage still show unfinished surfaces, as if straight from the quarry. Those within the Palazzo, by contrast, are finished smoothly, like the plaster surfaces they adjoin. Those in the grotto are immured in walls formed of shells, stones, and the irregular ground of the local landscape—nearly unformed (or formed roughly). The surfaces of the *cortile* mix these conditions, partly, it seems, because Romano anticipated the influence of the Mantua environment. The palace was built in the country with surfaces finished artificially with two ends in mind: to resist the deteriorating influence of the environment and to make surfaces appear as nature would have refinished them. Thus the Palazzo's smooth and rusticated surfaces, determined by both design and the circumstances of its rustic location, joined the city and country—artifice and nature—and by analogy effected the simultaneous completion and deformation of the construction. The building's regeneration and degeneration emphasizes the temporality of nature as an order of beginning and ending or, more broadly, life and death. These themes also appear in the fresco work on the building's interior. The relationship between an architectural surface of this kind and its setting is evident in the use of the term "rustic" to describe not only the site but the style.

The Rustic was so important to Vasari that it replaced the Tuscan as the simplest or "rudest" of the orders.[14] It was

Palazzo del Tè (1526)
Giulio Romano
Mantua, Italy

Palazzo del Tè (1526)
Giulio Romano
Mantua, Italy

The first rusticall workes were made in this manner, that is, péeces of stone roughly hewen out; but the ioyning together were proportionably made.

After, they deuided the stones in more proportion and shew, with flat lists, and for more beautie, and for ornaments sake made these crosses in them.

Other workemen brought in wrought Diamonds, and made them decently in this manner.

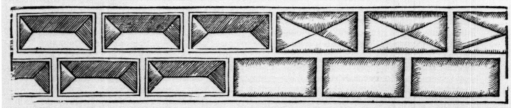

And in processe of time, things altered: workemen, for flat Diamonds, set flat tables, and raysed them somewhat higher, as in this figure is to be séene.

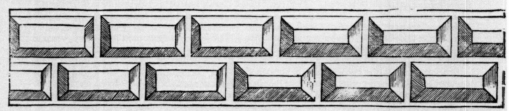

Some other workemen vsed more differences and séemelyer worke, neuerthelesse, all such workes haue their originall from rusticall worke, which is yet commonly called, Workes with poynts of Diamonds.

Héere endeth the maner of Thuscan worke, and now followeth
the order of Dorica.

Rustication
from Sebastiano Serlio, *Five Books on Architecture*, book 4

an appropriate mode of construction for walls that were to have a rough appearance, such as fortress or city walls. In rusticated masonry the sides of the stones in contact with each other were to be "dressed smooth" but the face of each stone was to project beyond the plane of the wall. Projections of this sort could be either rough and irregular or smooth and regular.

Leaving stones rough saved time and effort in construction, which seems to have motivated the use of rustic construction in antiquity, when its use was ubiquitous. Sometimes it appeared on temple podia, other times as fire walls. The most common usage was in Claudian architecture, for example in the huge wall of his temple platform on the Caelian Hill and in the Porta Maggiore, both of travertine. Rustication was also used on the whole face of buildings.

In the Renaissance, rustication became a dominant motif on the face of buildings—such as the Pitti or the Strozzi palace. The best example of this, perhaps, is Bramante's unfinished Tribunal on the Via Giulia in Rome. This usage was not only utilitarian, however; rustication was also used expressively. In Alberti's Palazzo Rucellai there is a discrepancy between the actual blocks used in the construction of the facade and the rusticated ashlar surface.[15] The prominent lines of the facade have been cut deeply and do not always coincide with the actual joints between blocks. Here the *appearance* of rustication

Palazzo Medici-Riccardi (1444)
Michelozzo di Bartolommeo
Florence, Italy

Palazzo del Tribunale (1512)
Donato Bramante
Rome, Italy

Palazzo Rucellai (1446–1451)
Leon Battista Alberti
Florence, Italy

Palazzo Rucellai (1446–1451), wall construction
Leon Battista Alberti
Florence, Italy
from B. Preyer, *Giovanni Rucellai*

Palazzo Rucellai (1446–1451), wall detail
Leon Battista Alberti
Florence, Italy

Palazzo Zuccaro (1579)
Federico Zuccaro
Florence, Italy

is being used to mask and correct construction. For Alberti there were expressive meanings associated with rustication; he described its rugged and threatening aspect.[16] Further, large rough-hewn stones were thought to add dignity to a building. He also recommended that the hardest and most irregular stones be placed at the bottom of walls. This was given ethical application in his essay "The Temple," where the stones at the bottom of a temple's foundation became indignant at their "unjust" treatment and "lowly" position and decided to rise up and revolt against the stones unfairly placed "above" them. The consequence of their "foolish" revolution was the collapse and ruin of the entire temple. This prompted Alberti's observation: "Anyone who does not know his place is mad."[17]

This injunction against misplacement did not prevent later architects, including Alberti himself, from using rustication in all parts of buildings and in combination with smooth surfaces. In the Palazzo del Tè the juxtaposition of smooth surfaces with coarse *rustica* was seen by Serlio as effecting a mixture and contrast of works of nature and artifice.[18] This mixture was commonplace in mannerist architecture. Gombrich brought this duality between art and nature within the parameters of modern psychology by utilizing the terms "reason" and "libido" in his seminal articles on the Palazzo del Tè.[19]

The expressive value of rustication was also known to early modern architects. Otto Wagner used rusticated granite to form the base of the outer surface of Vienna's Karlsplatz Station. Relatively thin panels of granite were attached to a load-bearing frame.[20] In forming the joints between load-bearing and cladding materials Wagner acknowledged not only the representational character of rustication by emphasizing the thinness of the stone but also its durable qualities. In St. Leopold's church at Steinhof, however, the traditional appearance of rustication was achieved in part through the subversion of traditional technique. Horizontal bands that mark the joints between pieces of marble cladding have been made to protrude beyond the facade surface, reversing what was traditionally a deep groove. Moreover, windows cut into the facade break the lines of these bands in such a way that the marble panels are shown to be thin and non-load-bearing, which contradicts the utilitarian purpose of rustication. What appears similar to a traditional form of construction is actually quite different. This is particularly evident in the use of bolts to hold the cladding panels onto the load-bearing brick wall. They reveal the thinness of the panels, even their lightness, but at the same time bear the marks of the building's duration. As cladding has become dominant in contemporary production this raises a question about the manner in which it is to respond to ambient weather conditions and the possibilities of weathering.

Karlsplatz, Hofpavillon (1894–1901), column base
Otto Wagner with Josef Olbrich
Vienna, Austria

Anstaltskirche Heilig Leopold (1903–1913)
Otto Wagner
Vienna, Austria

Postsparkasse (1904–1906)
Otto Wagner
Vienna, Austria

"De Telegraaf" (1927–1930)
J. F. Staal, G. J. Langhout
Amsterdam, Netherlands

How is an architectural surface affected by the action of the ambient elements? Consider first the flat surfaces of early modern buildings. Flatness in these buildings was invariably achieved through the application of a thin surface material to a load-bearing structure, the adhesion between them being what determined the duration of the outer construction. By contrast, the use of brick and stone in buildings both modern and ancient increases the thickness of surfaces exposed to the elements. Greater thickness usually results in longer durability, the latter being proportioned to the former. Erosion of a surface through weathering exposes newer surfaces of the same material in its depth, at once the erasure of one surface and the revelation of another. Exposure also involves sedimentation and the gathering of residual deposits, the combination of which—subtraction and addition—is a testimony to the time of the building, "creating the present form of a past life, not according to the contents or remnants of a past life but according to its past as such."[21] In this sense, architectural duration implies a past that is caught up in the present and anticipates the future.

Paradoxically, weathering produces something already there by subtraction. This exchanges the roles of art and nature. In design, art is assumed to be the power or agency that *forms* nature; in the life or time of a construction, however, nature *re-forms* the "finished" art work. When this formative

Maison Tzara (1925–1927)
Adolf Loos
Paris, France

Bartholomeus Ruloffstraat housing (1922–1924)
J. F. Staal
Amsterdam, Netherlands

Edifici residenziali nel Giardino Sola-Busca (1924–1930)
Aldo Andreani
Milan, Italy

Métro Porte Dauphine (1898–1901)
Hector Guimard
Paris, France

process is allowed to continue uninterrupted the surface of the original can be covered so completely that it disappears altogether under a patina, a time-bound "growth of skin"[22] that covers the new surface with an accumulation that represents the tension between a work of art and the conditions of its location. This differs from the imitation of organic forms in architecture, in art nouveau buildings for example, insofar as these buildings attempt to *look like* natural elements, whereas surface modification results from the *action of* these elements. In art nouveau buildings the accent is placed on *literal* imitation, neglecting the reflective distance that would allow for *mimesis*, as in earlier examples of arabesque and grotesque figuration.

What is the value of this accumulated dirt, or this erosion of a finished edge? Is it not tragic? Alternatively, does it not show the rightful claim nature has on all works of art? Is not this return of matter to its source, as a coherent body, already implied in its constitution, insofar as every physical thing carries within its deepest layers a tendency toward its own destruction—death as a birthright? If tragic, this metamorphosis is just. The value, then, of works that suffer stains and abrasions is the revelation of the eventuality of this final justice. This is the actual assimilation of an art work *back* into its location, the place *from which* it was first taken. In the time after construction, buildings take on the qualities of the place wherein they are sited, their colors and surface textures being

Hôtel Guimard (1909–1910)
Hector Guimard
Paris, France

Palazzo Castiglione (1901–1904)
Giuseppe Sommaruga
Milan, Italy

modified by and in turn modifying those of the surrounding landscape.

Dirt and staining: can they be anticipated? Certainly they are inevitable, but can they be projected, or envisaged as a likely future occurrence; still further, can they be incorporated into a design project? Staining is often the result of the juxtaposition of two materials, stone and metal for example, as in many nineteenth-century industrial buildings. When copper oxidizes and is washed by rain, a green stain is formed on the surface of the stone directly below. Stains seep into the porous stone, altering and deforming the original surface with these permanent markings. This may seem to be a deviation from the original intention for the surface color and texture, and it may be construed to have resulted from a *fault* in the design; but to the degree that stains show a new encounter between previously unrelated materials in one building sited in a particular place, they might also allow for a discussion of its harmony.

Staining, erosion, and surface faults seem to be antithetical to the modern movement's ideal of "whiteness." Le Corbusier, in "The Law of Ripolin: A Coat of Whitewash," faults the miser in us, exemplified by the character of Harpagon in Molière's *L'Avare*, the collector of material possessions.[23] This law was put forth as a critique of the house as a museum or temple "filled with votive offerings turning [the mind] into

Immeuble d'habitation (1902–1904)
Auguste Perret
Paris, France

"Lararium," Duchess Street (c. 1800)
Thomas Hope
London, England

a concierge or custodian." White Ripolin walls would resist the accumulation and accretion of "dead things" on their surfaces, as these would leave "marks," whereas on decorated walls, covered with damask or patterned wallpaper, these marks would be invisible. Observing that accretions do mark and preserve events from the past, Le Corbusier nevertheless recommended as more lively and accurate pure memory, which he understood to be recollection without the hindrance of intermediary dead objects: "The law of Ripolin would bring the joy of life, the joy of action. Solon, give us the law of Ripolin." This would represent the preservation of a balanced, harmonious structure, as existed in the cities Le Corbusier had visited on his travels. He lamented the likely disappearance of this traditional surface as a consequence of the westernization of older eastern cities and the industrial production of decorative elements—"dead things." Traditionally stones had been burnt, crushed, and thinned with water and applied to surfaces, making an "extraordinarily beautiful white." Le Corbusier made this "traditional" white the characteristic of the "modern," through the sacrifice of the stone to yield light (white). The aim was not to make the modern look like the traditional, but to make it an architecture of social justice and equality, transcending class barriers, an emblem of liberation within architecture.

The surfaces of the new buildings were to be not only "white" but also unified, planar, smooth, and "flat," masking the internal load-bearing structure but also revealing by contrast the outline of things, their volume and color, as absolute, without the possibility of mistake. Whiteness was taken to signify honesty and dependability. The morality of whitewash—an X ray of beauty—thus assumes a liberating force. Whiteness, the wealth of the rich and the poor, unites all classes, like bread and water; it is what all men need and what they enjoy. Anything "put on it" that was dishonest would "hit you" in the eye. Objects "stand forth" from white surfaces; lacking this ground no distinct figures can emerge. The white surface was thought to be the basis of objectivity and of "truth"; it is "the eye of truth." Le Corbusier observed this principle in his own work and found it in that of other architects. In praise of the architecture of Adolf Loos, Le Corbusier wrote that he "swept right beneath our feet, and it was a Homeric cleaning—precise, philosophical, and logical. In this, Loos has had a decisive influence on the destiny of architecture."[24] The precision being alluded to here parallels the X ray of white beauty in the law of Ripolin.

Loos, however, thought about whiteness differently; in his explanation of the white stucco surface of the Michaelerhaus in Vienna he argued that the architecture of every city has its own special character, Vienna's being lime wash.[25]

Sultan Mahembe and his two sons
from Le Corbusier, *The Decorative Art of Today*
"Three black heads against a white background, fit to dominate . . . an open door
through which we can see true grandeur"

Whiteness in this case was a result of local culture and regional construction, not, as it was for Le Corbusier, a beautiful and objective architectural finish for all locations. The difference amounts to a distinction between a background against which objects are revealed and a mask through which objects are partially disclosed.

This is particularly evident in consideration of the interiors of Le Corbusier and Loos. The interiors of Le Corbusier's buildings of the 1920s and 1930s—villas Stein and Savoye for example—present the same white on the interior as on the exterior, thus continuing the role of white as an "objective architectural finish." Continuous white also sustained the ideal of continuous space "flowing" inside and out. Within this space, standardized "household equipment" was to find its place. In *Precisions* Le Corbusier urged that the "equipment of the modern dwelling" replace traditional furniture, that "cabinets" and "containers" be mass-produced and made available to both architects and clients. While mass production would eliminate the dominance of cabinetmaker's furniture, it would also result in the lamentable loss of good craftsmen; yet for Le Corbusier this was inevitable if architects were to adapt themselves to "modern" times. Cabinets were to be placed within or alongside walls, thus leaving the space of the interior open by effectively emptying the house of its furniture. Equipment, so conceived, was intended for normal, typical, generalized

Looshaus, Michaelerplatz (1909–1911)
Adolf Loos
Vienna, Austria

occupants, serving standard and precise functions, put in order at human dimensions. "Farewell the chests of yesteryear." Le Corbusier intended interiors for neither this nor that particular person, but for a whole culture.

While he may have intended the same result, Loos approached the problem differently. Reminiscing about the interiors of his youth Loos observed that he did not grow up in a "stylish" home. Not a work of art, the house was his family's product. "It was our table, *ours!*" So, too, for the other furnishings: the writing table with the ink stain, the picture of his parents, the clock in the knit slipper, and so on. Every piece of furniture and object told a story, all together they narrated family history. As a result, the house was never finished, "it grew along with us and we grew within it." It possessed neither style, strangeness, nor *age,* in the sense of being typical of a particular period. What "style" it did have was that of Loos's family, a "style" that changed over time as did the family. The furnishings of Loos's apartment in Vienna illustrate this too. The space around the fireplace is *filled* with all manner of furniture: tables, stools, chests, sofas, and smaller objects such as pictures, books, clocks, etc., arranged to make the interior comfortable. These fittings were personal and peculiar to Loos; another inhabitant would have filled the space with others. And such a person would not have to be an architect to specify the right fittings.

Immeuble rue Vavin (1911)
Henri Sauvage
Paris, France

Loos's argument implied a rejection of the dictatorial manner in which "stylish" homes had been decorated in the past. This position was articulated forcefully in "Poor Little Rich Man." Regardless of approved taste, interiors were to be built up by owners themselves, making each interior individual and unique, as were its inhabitants. Such an interior would age with the family, changing as it does, yet sedimenting the past in the "present." This being said, it is also true that Loos, like Le Corbusier, was certainly aware of the tension between the private and public realms, as is attested in the indebtedness of the interiors of both architects to their respective cities of Vienna and Paris.

Implied in Le Corbusier's understanding of the white building is a finality that manifests itself upon the completion of a construction, although anticipated at the beginning of the project. Accordingly, the duration that is to follow the completion of the building—the life of the building—is conceived as a subtraction from the ideal condition of the project realized before inhabitation and weathering. It is in this sense that staining and erosion can be seen as an antithesis to the ideality of the project.

One might see in the modern movement's fascination with photography a desire to capture this moment of the complete project in spite of its inevitable transformation under the elements and through use. The black and white photo-

Villa Stein–de Monzie (1926–1928)
Le Corbusier
Garches, France

graph, in its high contrast between light, dark, and shade, was the ideal "trap" to capture permanently this fleeting figure. It is well known that Le Corbusier arranged and composed the ordinary domestic objects of his interiors for photographic purposes, giving the appearance of a scene frozen in time—a still life. This point is substantiated further by the dream of the empty space powerfully captured in the photographs of the house of Wittgenstein's sister; or similarly, the photographs of Mies's Barcelona Pavilion, which have served as the sole source of so many interpretations.[26]

But the very concept of the white or *the new* is part of a modern mentality that sees these in juxtaposition to *the old*, quite simply, that which has lasted. The romantic appreciation of "aging" referred to above can be related to a sense of the new versus the old that attributes positive value to the latter simply because it has lasted and stands as a *representation* of the past. Alois Riegl elaborated this pairing of the new and the old in his studies of architectural monuments, studies worked out when the modern architects of his generation were confronting the implications of these topics in the construction of their buildings.[27] His discussion of "age value" can be identified with the notion of aging as enhancement and the idea that the various markings and layers of a surface record and allow one to recollect earlier stages in the history of a building and the human life associated with it. The purity of the modern—

House of Mme R. (1927)
Robert Mallet-Stevens
Paris, France
Photo: Frank Yerbury
© AA London

newness—disavows this sense of recollection through association. This disavowal was made manifest in surfaces that were
not supposed to weather.

Whiteness, purity, and newness: what meanings were
associated with stains on buildings with these characteristics?
Given the desire for purity, whiteness, and newness, how can
modern architects have thought of inevitable stains on their
buildings as anything other than defilement?

Inherent in the title of Le Corbusier's reflections on the
United States, *When the Cathedrals Were White*, is the desire and
wish for whiteness. According to Le Corbusier, contemporary
cathedrals had not yet been built and the old ones belonging
to the dead were "blackened by soot and eaten away by wear
and tear."[28] Now soiled, cathedrals should be made white
again. Such a return would restore a time when thought was
clear, spirit alive, and the "spectacle clean." Already in his
Purism articles Le Corbusier praised the absence of distracting
marks as the precondition for the "play of masses in the light."
Such a play revealed primary architectural order, the "clear
thinking" and "living spirit" alluded to in the description of
"white cathedrals." While surfaces were redemptive and hygienic, just the opposite of dirt, soot, and grime, marks showing stain, defilement, and disorder. The white surface had a
bodily and spiritual charge. For Le Corbusier whiteness was a
matter of health, beauty, morality. Is there any better expla-

Nature morte à la pile d'assiettes (1920)
Le Corbusier
Basel, Switzerland

nation for the predominant images of cleanliness, isolation, and polish in his publications: the white decks of transatlantic liners in clean ocean air, the shiny, unused, unsoiled machine parts and all other mechanisms of faultlessness—airplanes, tools, highways, etc.? For modern architects, stains, such as those that resulted from surface accumulation of dirt, were thought of as *faults*, to be suppressed both technically and morally.

The fascination with whiteness and cleanliness is exemplified in the striking appearance of so many designs for hospitals, sanatoria, and other institutions that serve the health and hygiene of the citizens: the projects of Tony Garnier, Wagner, Hoffmann, Le Corbusier, and Aalto. Also indicative are the domestic interiors of these architects, the best-known example of which is the bathroom in Le Corbusier's Villa Savoye.

But is there not another sensibility at work in the construction of this room's surfaces—*color*? What role does color play in the designs of an architect who wants to make white buildings? In Le Corbusier's Purism articles color was treated under the category of "secondary elements," subordinate to the play of masses in light, an "enrichment grafted" onto white volumes, without which an artifact would be "denuded" of all sufficient "human resonance."[29] Color was seen as an addition to the white surface; although neither primary nor precise, it

The *Aquitania*
from Le Corbusier, *Towards a New Architecture*

Sairaala Tuberculosis Sanatorium (1928–1933)
Alvar Aalto
Paimio, Finland

Villa Savoye (1928–1931), bathroom
Le Corbusier
Poissy-sur-Seine, France

was necessary—a slight thickening that gave the surface depth. Perhaps the best example of this is the elaborate color scheme for the Pessac housing project, which was illustrated in *Oeuvre Complète* in dual fashion as *"peinte—non peinte."*

Fernand Léger went further than Le Corbusier in elaborating the necessity of surface color in architecture. He wrote: "The modern architect . . . has gone too far, in his magnificent attempts to cleanse through emptiness." Furthermore, "The thrust toward utility does not prevent the advent of a state of beauty."[30] As early as 1923 Léger had argued for the use of applied polychromy in architecture, where color was not subordinated to mass but seen as its necesssary complement, to counteract "the dissonance of modern living," as he argued one year later. Such was also the opinion of other artists and architects in the early 1920s. The research into the qualities of materials in the work of Mies van der Rohe and the similar preoccupation in the interiors of Loos also exemplify this tendency.[31] In all these cases, polished or white architecture is supplemented by one of color and material richness. This is not applied polychromy; materials are worked as substances that possess as a fact of their very depth the possibility of revealing the colors and textures of the earth, rather than those of paint or thin decorative elements.

This shift in aesthetic sensibility becomes evident in Le Corbusier's work in the late 1920s with his greater commit-

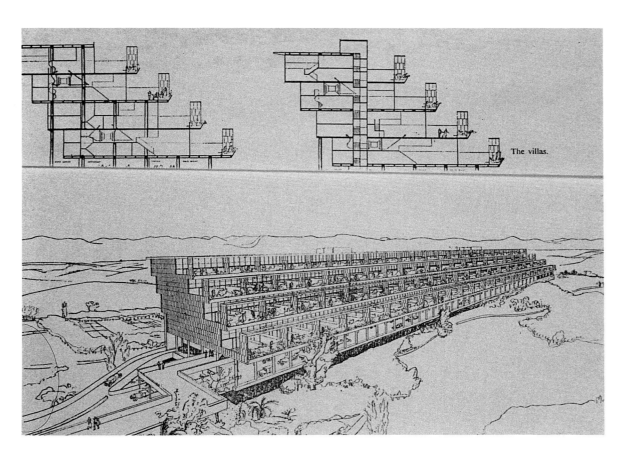

The villas.

Domaine Durand (1933–1934)
Le Corbusier
Algiers, Algeria

ment to what has been termed an "organic aesthetic," resulting in a parallel concern with issues of climate and topography.[32] His visits to distant lands, especially those in the colonies, allowed him to recognize climatic differences and the importance of determining the uniqueness of each as part of architectural design. Color led him from considerations of whiteness to materials, and materials led him from textures to the earth and climate. The unbuilt designs for the Domaine Durand in Algiers of 1933–1934, where Le Corbusier developed his concept of the *brise-soleil*, is symptomatic of his attention to the role of climatic conditions. In the Domaine Durand project the use of the stepped section and extended roof plane was to provide shaded areas for the apartments below, as well as circulation of air from the covered side through the whole apartment to terraces on the other side, which were wide enough for planting and were shaded by a disengaged bridgelike sunscreen. For Le Corbusier the use of the *brise-soleil* on the facades was to constitute a fundamental element of a new regional architecture of North Africa.

The use of the *brise-soleil* is a poignant example of the reinterpretation of a traditional element, the window within the wall. This reinterpretation seems to have been motivated by the newly invented "flat wall" and the problems it caused in hot weather, exemplified by the Salvation Army building during summer. The incorporation of the *brise-soleil* as an in-

Millowners' Association Building (1954)
Le Corbusier
Ahmedabad, India

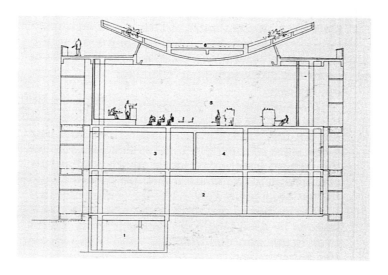

Millowners' Association Building (1954)
Le Corbusier
Ahmedabad, India

separable part of the facade of the Millowners' building and other similar projects led to the discovery of a new architectural facade: an exterior limit with a depth of an occupiable thickness, revealing a section of the inside on the outside. The enigmatic shadows of these facades are particularly evident in the buildings in India, where the play between the inside and the outside was so important that it changed the way buildings were defined—no longer was the outer wall the final limit of the space of the project; the building was interlocked with the ground. The hard and closed glass edge of the building box that led to the invention of the *brise-soleil* was eventually dissolved by it.

In sum, reinterpretation worked as follows: first, criticism and rejection of the thick wall and window well; second, development of the flat wall and expansive window (with conditioned air behind); third, recognition of consequent problems in hot weather; fourth, the invention of the sunscreen; and fifth, the discovery of a space—the space between the inside and the outside—that resulted from a new facade element. Reinterpretations of this sort are inventions that augment reality because they are productive, unlike designs that faithfully preserve the appearance of traditional elements in shape and profile through new materials. Similarly, the inverted roof of the Millowners' building became a receptacle garden providing an inhabitable and partially shaded terrain that allowed light to enter the main hall below. This part of the building is more interesting for its iconography (paradise garden, bull's horn, river section) than for its thermal properties and effects. Nevertheless, in these projects consciousness of weathering is a window through which concrete architectural conditions are both understood and reinvented.

The distinction to be observed is between adding to or subtracting from a given condition and attempting to reproduce the appearance of the same condition. Seen accordingly, the work of Carlo Scarpa, at least in its details, is a demonstration of the creative transformation of traditional elements. His projects for the Banca Popolare di Verona and the chapel in the Brion cemetery are examples of reinterpretation. At the bottom of each of the circular windows of the Verona bank is a vertical line running in the direction of the likely flow of rainwater. These lines demonstrate the possible effects of rainwater on the building's surface as they retard its effects; a virtual drip has been formed as an element of actual retardation that "reveals" what it removes and retards what it quickens. The likelihood of a mark of this sort was no doubt well known to Scarpa, as it is a commonplace on the facades of Venetian buildings. In the Brion cemetery, the tall, blank exterior wall of the chapel has become a setting for showing the effects of weathering in a dramatic manner. Scarpa interrupted the horizontal run of the stepped parapet with a gap that has allowed

Banca Popolare di Verona (1974–1981)
Carlo Scarpa
Verona, Italy

Banca Popolare di Verona (1974–1981), window
Carlo Scarpa
Verona, Italy

Santa Maria dei Miracoli (1481–1489)
Pietro Lombardo
Venice, Italy

Brion-Vega Cemetery (1970–1981)
Carlo Scarpa
San Vito di Altivole, Italy

the rainwater to seep through, leaving a black stain in the middle of the wall. This marking reveals, through weathering, nature's temporality; the beginning and end of things.

A simple cornice and a blank wall: is the mark a stain? Should it be cleaned? It seems possible to argue that Scarpa designed the blank (white) wall as the possibility for showing the life of the building in time, which was a creative reinterpretation of the fact of weathering.

Why would Scarpa or any other architect intentionally provide the means through which stains would appear? Seeing stains as aesthetic deformities calls for their complete elimination. Dirt, filth, grime, stains: must they not be removed? Do they not infect? Why set up the possibility of contagion? Removal will be seen as necessary as long as all stains are seen as signs of a deformation of an intended pure state. But dirt is not necessarily impure, buildings are made out of matter, earth is part of their fabric.

Can one not distinguish sediments or deposits that taint from those that do not? Surely this is a matter of intention and circumstance. In the Brion cemetery wall an element of everyday building deterioration has been used deliberately as a device for marking and infecting the purity of the new building surface. This intended marking can be distinguished from other cases of sediments or tainting insofar as it has been singled out or framed as unique.

Another example of intending weathering is the use of weathering steel in contemporary architecture. When exposed to the elements, weathering steel (Cor-Ten) rusts. Its surface color changes to earthy red, the evenness of which cannot be produced artificially. The speed of this process varies from place to place and is dependent upon both atmospheric and geographic conditions as well as the season of the year. The rusty patina that develops within a few months grows darker in time. The oxide surface is supposed to resist further corrosion and preserve the structural strength of the steel. If any part of its surface is scratched off, it reforms itself in time. Cleaning Cor-Ten promotes corrosion.

Cor-Ten, a high-strength, low-alloy steel, was first used in the John Deere Headquarters office building (1964) by Eero Saarinen and later by Roche and Dinkeloo in the Ford Foundation and Knights of Columbus buildings. The columns, girders, purlins, sun shades, and wall sections of the John Deere building are all made of weathering steel. Saarinen found this material to have maintenance-free characteristics. Cor-Ten was also appreciated for its appearance, its dark and expressive qualities.[33]

As a consequence of its surface transformation, weathering steel stains. It is not to be used next to white marble, block or cast concrete; better are surfaces covered with enamel or porcelain. This was one of the reasons, it seems, that Saari-

John Deere & Co. Headquarters (1963)
Eero Saarinen
Moline, Illinois

Coliseum
Kevin Roche, John Dinkeloo
New Haven, Connecticut

nen used weathering steel as comprehensively as possible—to reduce the possibility of staining. This helped the uniformity of the texture of the building, which was intended to blend into its surroundings. The building was seen not as an object placed on a site but as one that "grew from" its site. This repeats the theme of "organic architecture"; for Saarinen and the Taliesen group, including Wright himself, the bonding of a building to its place often involved overcoming the traditional distinction between the level of the land and that of the building, resulting in the absence of a single datum and the apparent emergence of the building from its place—"not upon but with" the topography.[34] Wright also saw a relationship between the composition of buildings and natural elements; in organic architecture the parts of a building were to be related to one another as were those of a plant, tree, or any other natural thing. Architecture, then, was conceived not as the building alone but in terms of its relationships to its surroundings, whether natural or man-made. This is also part of Saarinen's belief in the creation of a total environment, which does not imply the surrendering of the building to its place but instead the enhancement of place.

The organicism of this approach seems opposed to Le Corbusier's early fascination with whiteness and the desire to reveal objects against a whitewashed background. The first intends material expression, the second dematerialization and

Taliesin West (1938)
Frank Lloyd Wright
Paradise Valley, Arizona

consequent democratization. Poor construction of "white" buildings often led to their functional and aesthetic deterioration. This raises particularly difficult questions about their conservation and preservation. Given the desired ideality of dematerialization, should buildings of this sort always be preserved? Is it not false to envisage the life of a building as something that extends in perpetuity, something that must indefinitely bear the burden of its history? Would not a sense of the "end" of a construction envisage its final outline? Some buildings may be imagined to have a relatively limited lifespan, while others, because they are intended as permanent, may be realized perfectly *in* time through a series of sequential interventions.

The mouth kisses, the mouth spits; no one mistakes the saliva of the first for the second. Similarly, there is nothing necessarily impure about dirt. What must be determined are the conditions under which a surface marking is experienced as a stain. In traditional cultures the distinction between purity and impurity was not absolute, nor was that between what was sacred and profane; the relationship was ambiguous, each side of the pair being part of the other—dirt was *both* impure and pure. Since the eighteenth century we have come to see the gradual separation of these categories; Laugier, for example, called for the separation of cemeteries from the city, places for the dead being sites of impurity in contrast with hygienic urban locations. Le Corbusier was part of this Enlightenment tradition; his proposals for the city, especially the City of Three Million Inhabitants, reinforced the separation of these categories. Within this tradition, marks on white buildings will always be construed as stains, and impurities as faults.

In contrast to this, Le Corbusier's buildings in rough concrete represent another tradition, one in which marks are seen to be inevitable and the building is not intended to be or remain white. The expectation of weathering and poor workmanship in remote locations allowed Le Corbusier to use materials that could simultaneously hide the deficiencies of construction and reveal through their surface texture unintended weathering marks that added to the building. Faults were expected and served as the unexpected basis for new solutions. At the same time, in buildings built this way the likely residual deposit of dirt, and the sense of disorder it suggests, was anticipated and seen as part of the architectural order. Stains were not intended as elements of a fragmentary or fragmented architecture, instead their incorporation into the building added to its completeness. This way of building was later used in other locations where workmanship was more skilled, to the effect that weathering marks were seen as part of the finish of the building—even though this finish developed over time. The importation of these ideas, however, resulted in additional faults, as demonstrated in the relocation of ele-

Villa Shodhan (1951–1956)
Le Corbusier
Ahmedabad, India

ments and concepts of the Millowners' building, suited to the climate of Ahmedabad, in the form of the Carpenter Center for the Visual Arts, sited in Cambridge, Massachusetts. Le Corbusier is reported to have said that the concrete work of the Carpenter Center was too finely finished.

Weathering marks the passage of time. This time is not the moment of a pre-occupancy photograph; time's passage in architecture includes a building's inception, construction, and inhabitation. The project, too, endures *through* these phases. In construing an architectural project the introduction and consideration of the time of weathering brings the project closer to a condition of actuality based on its potential trans-formations through time. This condition of actuality and po-tential for staining and fault complements the ideality of the project, making it both independent of the passage of time and caught up within it. Thought of in this way, weathering brings the virtual future of a building into dialogue with its actual present, as both are entangled in its past.

This temporal structure of building can be compared to a person's experience of time. At every moment in one's life earlier times of infancy, childhood, youth, and all other stages up to now are still present, increasing in number yet unchanged and familiar, and subject to redefinition and appropriation. Never is one's past not present, nor is the individual's past ever cut off from the tradition of one's culture and the time of

Carpenter Center for the Visual Arts (1961–1964)
Le Corbusier
Cambridge, Massachusetts

Museo di Castelvecchio (1957–1964)
Carlo Scarpa
Verona, Italy

Bartholomeus Ruloffstraat housing (1922–1924)
J. F. Staal
Amsterdam, Netherlands

the natural world. Duration invokes recollection in each of its advancing moments. The differentiation of the present (as something in itself) presumes the reality of the past as the context from which it has emerged. Every act preserves the coherence of temporal continuity against its theoretical disintegration into separate parts: past, present, and future. Yet one's sense of the past or of the future involves a reach out of the present into some time when it (one's present) was not yet, or some time when it will be no longer. Events in the past—at least our feelings, thoughts, tastes, and so on about them—"mark" the memory, like a signet on a "good thick slab of wax" said Socrates in *Theaetetus*. What remains from the past is a trace or impression of an event, not the thing itself as it existed when present. Likewise, mnemic experience in architecture is not of the present but of the past. The past in this sense is not a specific and limited period or time over and done with, rather it can be seen as "what has come to be."[35]

The fact of weathering inheres in all construction. No architect can avoid this fact; it was never escaped in the past, nor can it be in the present. Weathering reminds one that the surface of a building is ever-changing. While a potential nuisance, the transformation of a building's surface can also be positive in that it can allow one to recognize the necessity of change, and to resist the desire to overcome fate—an aspiration

Rue Mallet-Stevens (1926–1927)
Robert Mallet-Stevens
Paris, France

26 via Modrone
Milan, Italy

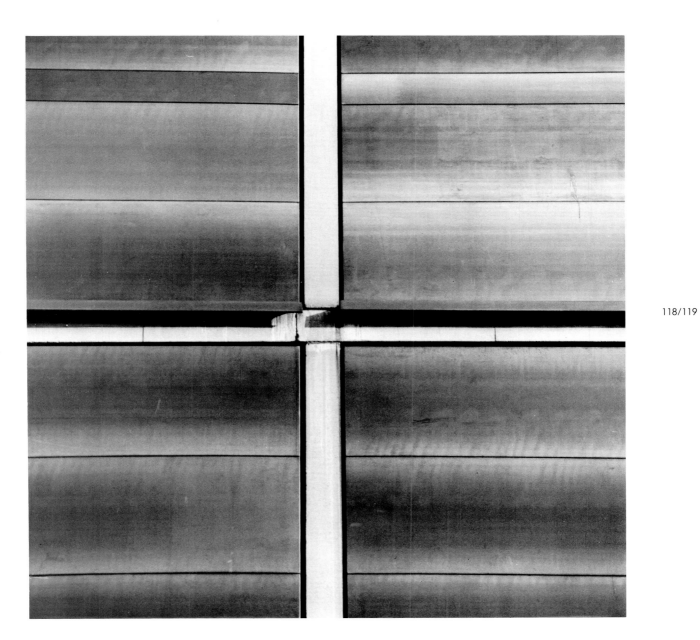

Yale Center for British Art (1969–1974)
Louis I. Kahn
New Haven, Connecticut

that dominated much of modernist architectural thought through its resistance to time. The preoccupation with the image or appearance of the building in current practice is in part symptomatic of this desire. Images are media of representation that communicate a building's style, character, and identity and are often thought to do so without change, like the printed word. This ironically vindicates Hugo: buildings have become like books because their images have attained the status of text, whether the text-image simulates historical buildings or not. What makes this ironic is that books themselves are "artifacts" that sustain multiple readings—as buildings always do.

The ideas of a project, hypothesized in sketches, drawings, and models, are its past, which will be soiled by the marks of weathering after construction. The effects of these marks can be retarded through inventive solutions. These solutions could be elements that direct or prevent the flow of water, or they could respond to the effects of the weather by creating situations that both recognize and utilize the ever-changing characteristics of materials as a way of renewing beginnings by allowing refinishing.

NOTES

Epigraph: Octavio Paz, *A Draft of Shadows* (New York, 1979), p. 171.

1. Victor Hugo, *Notre Dame de Paris,* book 5, ch. 2, "This Will Kill That," which gives Hugo's reference to the deteriorating yet unfinished Notre Dame, as well as his argument about the triumph of printing over architecture as the medium of cultural memory. This thesis is described fully in Neil Levine, "The Romantic Idea of Architectural Legibility: Henri Labrouste and the Neo-Grec," in *The Architecture of the Ecole des Beaux Arts,* ed. Arthur Drexler (New York, 1977), pp. 324–416. Hugo apparently asked the architect Henri Labrouste to review the chapter cited above. Labrouste's acceptance of Hugo's thesis is apparent in the facade of the Bibliothèque Sainte-Geneviève, as well as in his reconstruction drawings of Paestum.

    Hugo's thesis had ancient precedents. Plato, although less committed to an idea of writing as the primary instrument of cultural memory, wrote in *Phaedrus* 275d–e: "Writing, Phaedrus, has this strange power, quite like painting in fact; for the creatures in paintings stand there like living beings, yet if you ask them anything they maintain a solemn silence. It is the same with written words. You might imagine they speak as if they were actually thinking something but if you want to find out about what they are saying and question them, they keep on giving the same one message eternally."

2. Le Corbusier, *Towards a New Architecture* (New York, 1972), p. 13. Throughout Le Corbusier's text, the engineer is put forth as the source of an improved way of building and living, which would result in progress toward better conditions. On this argument, and

the role of the symbolism of the engineer in modern architecture more broadly, see Reyner Banham, *Theory and Design in the First Machine Age* (London, 1969), pp. 220–249. Banham discussed the *machine à habiter* and equated Le Corbusier's sense of "machine" design with "classical" architecture by elaborating the theory of "object-types." This material has been reviewed more recently in Manfredo Tafuri and Francesco Dal Co, *Modern Architecture* (New York, 1976), pp. 138ff.

Le Corbusier was obsessed with the theme of the machine: see his *Decorative Art of Today* (Cambridge, Mass., 1987), pp. 69–84 and 105–116; particularly relevant on the idea of the "machine" is the chapter "The Lesson of the Machine"; on the related theme of beautiful tools see "Type-Needs and Type-Furniture." The "machine" symbolism is enlarged to account for both an epoch and a state of mind in Le Corbusier, *Precisions* (Cambridge, Mass., 1991), pp. 23–34, "To Free Oneself Entirely of Academic Thinking," where thinking in the machine age is contrasted with practice in the "academy."

For a discussion of the impact of this body of ideas on Le Corbusier's built work see William Curtis, *Le Corbusier: Ideas and Forms* (New York, 1986).

The concrete possibilities of merging architectural thinking with mechanized production are described in Gilbert Herbert, *The Dream of the Factory-Made House: Walter Gropius and Konrad Wachsmann* (Cambridge, Mass., 1984).

3.   Banham, *Theory and Design in the First Machine Age*. See also Le Corbusier, *Precisions,* "Techniques Are the Very Basis of Poetry. They Open a New Cycle in Architecture," pp. 35–66.

4.   Sigfried Giedion, *Mechanization Takes Command* (New York, 1948), especially parts 5 and 6. This classic text documents the collision between mechanization and the lived world. The survey begins in the late Middle Ages and reviews topics near and far from architecture, the most relevant sections being those on furnishings and mechanization entering the household. A related, shorter and more philosophical text is Lewis Mumford's *Technics and Civilization* (New York, 1963), especially ch. 7, pp. 321–363, "Assimilation of the Machine," where Mumford emphasizes the machine as an instrument of conquest that has led to fundamental changes in the "mode of life."

5.   See Andrew Saint, *The Image of the Architect* (New Haven, 1983), which treats this development fully in its study of nineteenth-century architectural practice. A more comprehensive picture emerges in the chapters of Spiro Kostof, *The Architect* (Oxford, 1977). The current state of the problem is put forth in Robert Gutman, *Architectural Practice* (Princeton, 1988), and Dana Cuff, *Architecture: The Story of Practice* (Cambridge, Mass., 1991). Many useful observations on contemporary architectural practice are put forth in Donald Schon, *The Reflective Practitioner* (New York, 1982). Schon's chapter 3, entitled "Design as a Reflective Conversation with the Situation," is to the point but shows little consideration of the tension between the builder's and architect's knowledge of building production.

6.   William Mitchell, *Computer-Aided Architectural Design* (New York, 1977), especially pp. 27–65. Also useful is *The Computability of Design* (State University of New York at Buffao, 1986). The proceedings from this symposium on computer-assisted design addressed: "Models of Design," "Design Knowledge," "Computational Design Methods," and "Computer-Assisted Design."

7. Alvaro Siza y Vieira, *Alvaro Siza: Figures and Configurations,* ed. Wilfried Wang (New York, 1988), p. 5. The topic Siza has raised has been made part of a more inclusive theoretical framework in Kenneth Frampton, "Towards a Critical Regionalism: Six Points for an Architecture of Resistance," in Hal Foster, ed., *The Anti-Aesthetic: Essays on Postmodern Culture* (Port Townsend, Wash., 1983), pp. 16–30. Frampton has addressed Siza's work specifically in his contribution to Alvaro Siza, *Professione poetica — Poetic Profession* (Milan, 1986).

    An attempt to treat the philosophical implications of the problem of site specificity has been made in E. C. Relph, *Place and Placelessness* (London, 1978). Unfortunately, this attempt suffers from a restricted view of modern architecture. Fuller, but not much better on this account, are the books of Christian Norberg Schultz. In Norberg Schultz's *Meaning in Western Architecture* (New York, 1980), pp. 186–226, the limitations of "functionalist" reductions to "type" are shown to have led (in postmodern architecture) to a "pluralist" reaction generating regionalist or local responses that resulted in designs that characterize their locale. We shall show that this "reaction" has long been part of modern architecture.

8. Siza, *Alvaro Siza: Figures and Configurations.*

9. Le Corbusier, *Precisions* (Paris, 1930), pp. 64ff., cited in Reyner Banham, *Architecture of the Well-Tempered Environment* (Chicago, 1969), p. 159.

10. Ibid.; see also Le Corbusier, *When the Cathedrals Were White* (New York, 1947), p. 20.

11. Le Corbusier and Pierre Jeanneret, *Oeuvre Complète de 1929–1934* (Zurich, 1947), pp. 97ff.; see also Brian Brace Taylor, *Le Corbusier: The City of Refuge, Paris 1929–33* (Chicago, 1987), chs. 2–4, especially pp. 111–117. Le Corbusier's ideas were set forth most emphatically in *The Radiant City: Elements of a Doctrine of Urbanism to Be Used as the Basis of Our Machine-Age Civilization* (New York, 1967). This text shows particularly well the intermixing of semiscientific information with cosmological symbolism. Clean air, to name one of the most polyvalent of his topics, is presented as a "biological need" and the life force (*anima*) of the world.

12. R. B. White, *The Changing Appearance of Buildings* (London, 1967). This text demonstrates that the British climate, especially in London, has brought forth a "crop of ruined appearances" on buildings built between the 1930s and 1960s. Many examples of staining and "unsightliness" are shown and discussed, and the causes of surface marking are summarized.

13. Georg Simmel, "The Ruin," in *Essays on Sociology, Philosophy and Aesthetics* (New York, 1959), pp. 259–266. On Palazzo del Tè see Fredrick Hartt, *Giulio Romano* (New York, 1981), pp. 91–104; Kurt Forster and Richard Tuttle, "The Palazzo del Tè," *Journal of the Society of Architectural Historians* (1971), pp. 267–293; E. H. Gombrich, "Zum Werke Giulio Romanos," *Jahrbuch der Kunsthistorischen Sammlungen in Wien,* n.f., 8 (1934), pp. 79–104, and 9 (1935), pp. 121–150.

14. Giorgio Vasari, *On Technique* (New York, 1960), pp. 65ff. and pp. 132ff.; see also James Ackerman, "The Tuscan/Rustic Order: A

Study in the Metaphorical Language of Architecture," *Journal of the Society of Architectural Historians* (1983), pp. 15–34; Giulio Carlo Argan, *Studi e note dal Bramante al Canova* (Rome, 1970), p. 52; Erik Forsman, *Dorisch, Ionisch, Korinthisch: Studien über den Gebrach der Säulenordnungen in der Architektur des 16–18 Jahrhunderts* (Stockholm, 1961), ch. 1.

15. Brenda Preyer, "The Rucellai Palace," in F. W. Kent et al., *Giovanni Rucellai ed il suo Zibaldone II: A Florentine Patrician and his Palace* (London, 1981), pp. 155–228. Also useful is Franco Borsi, *Leon Battista Alberti: The Complete Works* (New York, 1981), pp. 51–56. The status of geometry—as an instrument and as symbolism—in Alberti's architecture is discussed in Rudolph Wittkower, Architectural Principles in the Age of Humanism (New York, 1962). An attempt to elaborate Wittkower's thesis can be found in George Hersey, *Pythagorean Palaces: Magic and Architecture in the Italian Renaissance* (Ithaca, 1976). The most recent thorough study of facades composed in the Renaissance according to geometric norms is contained in John Onians, *Bearers of Meaning: The Classical Orders in Antiquity, the Middle Ages and the Renaissance* (Princeton, 1988).

16. Leon Battista Alberti, *On the Art of Building in Ten Books,* translated and edited by Joseph Rykwert et al. (Cambridge, Mass., 1988), book 7, ch. 2. For an interpretation of this see Joseph Rykwert, ed., *Leonis Baptiste Alberti* (London, 1979). Particularly useful in this series of essays is Hubert Damisch, "The Column and the Wall," pp. 18–23.

17. Leon Battista Alberti, *Dinner Pieces* (Binghamton, 1987), pp. 175–176, "The Templum."

18. Sebastiano Serlio, *The Five Books of Architecture* (New York, 1982), book iv, fol. xi.

19. Gombrich, "Zum Werke Giulio Romanos." For more on this theme, see Marcello Fagiolo and Alessandro Rinaldi, "*Artifex et/aut Natura*: The Dialectic between Imitation and Imagination," *Lotus International* 32.

   The philosophical implications of this topic are elaborated in Ananda Coomaraswamy, "Ornament," in *Selected Papers: Traditional Art and Symbolism,* ed. Roger Lipsey (Princeton, 1985), pp. 241–253.

20. Edward Ford, *The Details of Modern Architecture* (Cambridge, Mass., 1990), pp. 211ff. This topic is studied in a different context in John Macsai and Paul Doukas, "Expressed Frame and the Classical Order in the Transitional Period of Italy, 1918–1939," *Journal of Architectural Education,* 40, no. 4, pp. 10–17, where the expressed frame and infill panel are shown to allow for ambiguous readings of the structural frame and suggestions of a load-bearing wall. Much more information and interpretation of the relationship between a structural frame and cladding has arisen in the study of early twentieth-century American architecture—especially the architecture of the "Chicago School." On this see Colin Rowe, "The Chicago Frame," in *Mathematics of the Ideal Villa and Other Essays* (Cambridge, Mass., 1985), pp. 90–117; Henrich Klotz, "The Chicago Multistory as a Design Problem," in *Metropolis* (Munich, 1987), pp. 56–75; William H. Jordy, *American Buildings and Their Architects,* vol. 3 (New York, 1972), especially the chapter entitled "Masonry Block and Metal Skeleton: Chicago and the 'Commercial Style'"; and J. Carson Webster, "The Skyscraper: Logical and Historical Considerations," *Journal of the Society of Architectural Historians,* 18 (1969), pp. 129–139.

21. Simmel, "The Ruin," p. 265.

22. Ibid.

23. Le Corbusier, *The Decorative Art of Today* (Cambridge, Mass., 1987), pp. 188–192. This text has been considered recently in Mark Wigley, "Architecture after Philosophy: Le Corbusier and the Emperor's New Paint," in "Philosophy and Architecture," *Journal of Philosophy and the Visual Arts* (London, 1990), pp. 84–95.

An equally clear image of whiteness appears in Duchamp's *Apolinere Enameled* (1916–1917).

Whiteness is, however, a quality with a broad range of meanings. Le Corbusier's sense of a "white wall" can be usefully compared to the "white wall of a whale" in Melville's *Moby Dick* (1851). Melville, in a chapter entitled "The Whiteness of the Whale," explained how "it was the whiteness of the whale that above all things appalled." Though whiteness may seem to enhance beauty and add some special virtue of its own; though it may seem to typify honesty, justice, purity, and royal preeminence—as in visions of spiritual and holy things—this quality can be divorced from these associations and coupled with terrible objects. Consequently, as in the case of the white whale, it may greatly heighten terror and dread. Whiteness in a large animal symbolizes its capacity to overpower: hence our profound fear of the white bear, shark, or tiger. And in humans whiteness is even more disturbing; Melville's Ishmael claims that the albino always repels, even if lacking any (other) physical deformity. Why is this so? Void of color and quality, white is the essence of emptiness and indefiniteness, a heartless abyss or silent absence awaiting us like death into which we plunge when all moorings are lost; whiteness is the thought of annihilation, an expansive blankness totally bereft of life—a monumental shroud otherwise named nothingness. Melville wrote that this is what appalled Ishmael.

The importance of whiteness in *Moby Dick* is described in John Borton, *Herman Melville: The Philosophical Implications of Literary Technique in Moby Dick* (Amherst, 1961), pp. 18–24.

24. Le Corbusier, "Adolf Loos," in *Frankfurter Zeitung* (1930), quoted in Benedetto Gravagnuolo, *Adolf Loos: Theory and Works* (Milan and New York, 1982), p. 89.

25. Adolf Loos, *Trotzdem* (Vienna, 1982), p. 111. The history of this case is put forth fully in Hermann Czech and Wolfgang Mistelbauer, *Das Looshaus* (Vienna, 1976), p. 197. The implications of this project on Loos's understanding of "whiteness" is elaborated in David Leatherbarrow, "Interpretation and Abstraction in the Architecture of Adolf Loos," *Journal of Architectural Education,* 40, no. 4 (Summer 1987), pp. 2–9. The subject is also reviewed in Gravagnuolo, *Adolf Loos.* All the documents relating to the project and resulting controversy are brought together in Burkhardt Rukschcio and Roland Schachel, *Adolf Loos: Leben und Werk* (Salzburg, 1982). The theme of whiteness and the related issue of newness are variously treated in a number of recent Loos studies; see particularly the collection brought together by Yehuda Safran and Wilfried Wang, eds., *The Architecture of Adolf Loos* (Arts Council of Great Britain, London, 1987).

26. Thomas Schumacher, "Deepspace/shallow space," *Architectural Review,* 181 (January 1987), pp. 37–42; see also Juan Pablo Bonta, *Architecture and Its Interpretation: A Study of Expressive Systems in Ar-*

chitecture (Barcelona, 1975), pp. 64ff. In this insightful text Bonta documents the difference between interpretations developed through knowledge from direct experience of a building—the Barcelona Pavilion in this case—and knowledge gained from photographs.

27. Alan Colquhoun, "'Newness' and 'Age Value' in Alois Riegl," in *Modernity and the Classical Tradition* (Cambridge, Mass., 1989), pp. 213–221; for Riegl, see "The Modern Cult of Monuments: Its Character and Its Origin," *Oppositions,* 25 (Fall 1982); further see Alan Colquhoun, "Thoughts on Riegl," *Oppositions* 25 (Fall 1982).

    The most recent, and in many respects challenging, philosophical study of this problem is Emmanuel Levinas, "The Old and the New," in *Time and the Other and Other Essays* (Pittsburgh, 1987), pp. 121–138.

    The nineteenth-century cultural background of Riegl's arguments is described in Xavier Costa, "Mercurial Markers: An Interpretation of Architectural Monuments in Early Nineteenth Century France," dissertation, University of Pennsylvania, 1990.

28. Le Corbusier, *When the Cathedrals Were White,* p. 5.

29. Le Corbusier and Amédée Ozenfant, "Purism," in *Modern Artists on Art,* ed. Robert Herbert (Englewood Cliffs, 1964), pp. 58–73. The impact these arguments had on built work can be seen in Le Corbusier and Pierre Jeanneret, *Oeuvre Complète, 1910–1929,* vol. 1 (Zurich, 1964). Especially interesting is the account of Pessac—the illustrations of the exterior surfaces painted and unpainted (pp. 78–85). Also relevant is Amédée Ozenfant, *Foundations of Modern Art* (New York,

1952), as well as the recent survey of this movement, Susan Ball, *Ozenfant and Purism: The Evolution of a Style, 1915–1930* (Ann Arbor, 1981), where the idea of white is related to both Purism and racism. The broader context is outlined in *Léger and Purist Paris* (Tate Gallery, London, 1970).

For comparison with related arguments raised in De Stijl see Yve-Alain Bois, *Painting as Model* (Cambridge, Mass., 1990), as well as the key document in the tradition it elaborates: Piet Mondrian, *Plastic Art and Pure Plastic Art* (New York, 1951).

30. Fernand Léger, *Functions of Painting* (New York, 1973), pp. 94, 53.

31. Mies van der Rohe, "Was wäre Beton, was Stahl ohne Spiegelglas?," cited in Fritz Neumeyer, *Mies van der Rohe, das kunstlose Wort* (Berlin, 1986), p. 378. On the qualities of materials in Mies's architecture see José Quetglas, "Fear of Glass: The Barcelona Pavilion," in *Architectureproduction* (New York, 1988), pp. 121–151. The details of Miesian construction have been redrawn in Edward Ford, *The Details of Modern Architecture* (Cambridge, Mass., 1990). This book also contains drawings of buildings by Loos, and for that comparison alone it merits study. On Loos, in addition to texts cited in note 25 above, see Adolf Loos, "Die Baumaterialien" and "Das Prinzip der Bekleidung," in *Ins Leere gesprochen* (Vienna, 1981), pp. 133–138 and pp. 139–145, and Max Risselada, ed., *Raumplan versus Plan Libre: Adolf Loos and Le Corbusier* (New York, 1988).

32. Mary McLeod, "Le Corbusier and Algiers," *Oppositions,* nos. 19–20 (Winter–Spring 1980). Further, see Frampton, "Towards a Critical

Regionalism," as well as Carlo Palazzolo and Riccardo Vio, eds., *In the Footsteps of Le Corbusier* (New York, 1991); and Peter Carl, "Natura Morta," in *Modulus,* 20 (1991), pp. 20–71.

33. Eero Saarinen, *Global Architecture* (Tokyo, 1971), on John Deere and Cor-Ten. This doctrine is evident in other works; for example, the Rocky Mountain National Park building by Edmond Casey of the Taliesen group was designed to harmonize with its surroundings.

34. Frank Lloyd Wright, *The Living City* (New York, 1958), p. 112. This text is the clearest of Wright's many attempts to describe the work of placing a building "on or in" its site (land); see also Frank Lloyd Wright, "The Meaning of Materials," in *In the Cause of Architecture* (New York, 1975), pp. 139–219. More recently this topic has been studied in cultural geography; see, for example, J. B. Jackson, *The Necessity for Ruins* (Amherst, 1980); as well as Denis Cosgrove, *Social Formation and Symbolic Landscape* (London, 1984).

35. David Farell Krell, *Of Memory, Reminiscence and Writing* (Bloomington, 1990), p. 14. Plato's account of memory is summarized fully and clearly in Jacob Klein, *A Commentary on Plato's Meno* (Chicago, 1989). The problem is cast in a historical perspective in Peter Munz, *The Shapes of Time* (Middletown, Conn., 1977); as well as George Kubler, *The Shape of Time: Remarks on the History of Things* (New Haven, 1962). Also useful is Edward Said, *Beginnings* (New York, 1985).

    Much recent reflection on memory elaborates phenomenological philosophy; see Erwin Straus, "Memory Traces," in *Phenomenological Psychology* (New York, 1966), pp. 75–100; Edward Casey, *Remem-*

bering: A Phenomenological Study (Bloomington, 1987); David Michael Levin, *The Body's Recollection of Being: Phenomenological Psychology and the Deconstruction of Nihilism* (Boston, 1985); David Carr, *Time, Narrative, and History* (Bloomington, 1986); and most important perhaps, Paul Ricoeur, *Time and Narrative,* 3 vols. (Chicago, 1984–1988).

ACKNOWLEDGMENTS

Most of the photographs for this publication were especially commissioned. We owe a great debt of gratitude to Charles Tashima for his meticulous attention to detail and his passion and perseverance on a journey that followed our imaginary grand tour. The office of former Dean Gerald M. McCue and Associate Dean Polly Price at the Graduate School of Design, Harvard University, and the University of Pennsylvania Faculty Research Foundation contributed to making the photographs possible.

The text was developed during a series of visits to Cambridge and Philadelphia. The delights of these brief meetings would not have been possible without the generous and giving support of Homa Fardjadi and Lauren Leatherbarrow. Peter Carl's insightful and attentive reading of the manuscript provided us with encouragement as well as helping to focus passages related to the work of Le Corbusier. There is further debt to our friends, teachers, and inspirators: Alan Colquhoun, Marco Frascari, Rafael Moneo, Alan Plattus, Joseph Rykwert, and Dalibor Vesely.